A World of Change

CHILDREN IN TUDOR ENGLAND

Tony Kelly

History Department, Dragon School, Oxford

Series editor: Rosemary Kelly

How to use this book 2
Home and school 3
Games and entertainments ... 15
Babies and toddlers 20
Apprentices and others 27
The Lisle family 33
A boy king – Edward VI. Born 1537, reigned 1547–53 41
Find out more for yourself 50
Index 51

This book is about the lives of children in Tudor England. We can find out about some famous children who lived then because letters and written descriptions, as well as portraits, have survived. But the great majority of Tudor children had parents who were neither well known, nor wealthy, and who certainly could not afford the cost of a portrait or the expense of books and writing materials. Many of them could not read or write anyway. To learn something of their daily lives we have to rely on evidence of a more general nature because there is very little to be found which tells us much about them as individuals. So this book is in two parts. The first part tells about some imaginary children in a less well-off household, and the evidence we have for the kind of life they led. The second part tells the story of some real children from well-known and important families about whom we have plenty of evidence.

Stanley Thornes (Publishers) Ltd

How to use this book

Lord and Lady Cobham and their family painted in 1567. Lord Cobham stands on the left, firmly in control of his large family. His wife, Frances, aged 25, is sitting by him, and her elder sister Jane is on the right. She is probably unmarried, and as she has no household of her own, has to live with her sister.
The children from left to right are: Maximilian aged two, Henry aged one, sitting on his mother's knee, William aged six, Elizabeth and Frances, twins of five, Margaret aged four.

Look at the picture above of the Cobhams and their children. They are quite a lucky family, because they have six children, close together in age. More children died in Tudor England than in our twentieth century – but even so families were usually larger than nowadays. Notice the fine clothes and jewellery, expensive pets, and the grand dishes. Remember that only wealthy families in the sixteenth century could afford to have their portraits painted. This picture gives us a great deal of evidence on what we might expect to find in other wealthy Tudor families.

The picture on the cover gives us different evidence. A sixteenth-century artist, Pieter Bruegel, painted it in the Netherlands. The children are not wealthy, and they are not posing for their portraits. They are playing ordinary everyday games just like children in England at that time.

But we must be on our guard about evidence. A writer on page 7 says that almost everywhere children are badly taught. He may have been right, but we should be suspicious about his reason for saying this, because we also know that he is the author of a school-book which he obviously wants to sell well to parents.

Look again at the Cobham picture. There they are, posing elegantly for their portrait, but this does not mean that they were always beautifully dressed and beautifully behaved. Imagine what might happen when the adults leave the room. Margaret lets go of the monkey. It promptly makes a dash for the parrot which knocks over the wine goblet. The twin on the left jogs her sister's arm and makes her drop her apple. The bird makes a mess on William's arm, and pecks two-year-old Maximilian's hand as he tries to grab a grape. To complete the chaos, the dog starts yapping and makes the baby cry!

When we try to imagine a situation like that, we are doing something else important. History is about real people in the past. The evidence tells us something of what the children did, but we must also try to understand what it felt like to wear clothes like theirs, to learn the things expected of them – and to grow up in Tudor England.

Home and school

'School, school, school!' grumbled Walter to himself, stretching and yawning as he slowly got out of bed. 'Every day the same – Latin, endless Latin, boring Latin...'

'Hurry up, Walter, you'll be late!' his mother's voice echoed up the stairs, interrupting his thoughts.

'There she goes again,' muttered Walter. 'It's all right for her and Kate – they haven't got to sit through hours and hours of old Carey droning on and on, and then pouncing on you with that birch of his when you forget something.' He moodily put on his shirt and hose, grabbed his doublet and ran downstairs, fumbling with the buttons and laces. He seized a piece of bread from the table at the same moment as his father came through from his shop. Still clutching the bread, Walter knelt in front of his father for his blessing.

'God keep you, Wat,' his father said, 'and, remember, run all the way to school – no dawdling – and don't forget your satchel as you did last week ... and make sure you've got your ink-horn and your quill pen... and have you still got plenty of paper? I hope so: remember it costs fourpence a *quire* [24 sheets] and I'm not made of money!'

'Yes, sir, it's all ready – I'll go straight off now,' and snatching his cap and gown Walter rushed out into the street. But he had not gone many yards before his sister Kate was shouting at him from the door: 'Don't forget, Master Carey is coming back to dinner with us today.' Walter waved his hand to show he had understood, though it was lucky his parents were not able to hear his muttered comments. It was bad enough to have to put up with his schoolmaster all day in the classroom, without having to bring him back for a meal in his own house as well.

School started at 7 a.m., and the church clock had already struck as Walter crept through the door and sidled into his place on the bench. Prayers had begun and Walter was quick to mumble with the others the Fifth Commandment that they were reciting: 'Honour thy father and thy mother; that thy days may be long in the land which the Lord thy God giveth thee.'

Prayers over, each boy was asked questions about the service he had attended the Sunday before; Walter was not looking forward to this ordeal.

'Were you present at the sermon, Walter?'

'I was present, sir.'

'At what time did the preacher start?'

'At 7 o'clock.'

'From where did he take his text?'

'Out of the Epistle of Paul to the Romans.'

'What chapter?'

'The eighth.'

'You have answered well so far; now let's hear what happened next. Have you remembered anything of the sermon?'

'Er, well – nothing that I can recite.'

'What do you mean? Can't you tell me anything at all about it?'

Walter then had to admit that he had been asleep or day dreaming for most of the sermon and that he 'deserved stripes'. Master Carey was inclined to agree with him, but Walter craftily reminded him that he had been invited back to the Procters' house for dinner and the schoolmaster relented. (He probably remembered the delicious pike and artichokes that he enjoyed the last time he dined at Walter's house.)

When Walter arrived at school, he would have walked into a schoolroom like this. The boys are all dressed like him in a doublet and hose, and the teachers wear long gowns. There are several different classes in the same room. How do the teachers keep order?

Reading and writing

Beginners at reading and writing were provided with a **horn book**. This was a sheet of paper, mounted on a board with a handle, on which the alphabet was printed. It was protected by a thin sheet of transparent horn. As you can see from the picture, the alphabet is printed first in small letters, then in capitals; then there are some simple combinations of letters, and the Lord's Prayer. After mastering these, the pupil started practising simple sentences such as 'Boy, go thy way to the top of the hill where the big tree is.'

A sixteenth-century horn book.

PRECEPTES OF WRITING.

The writer must prouide him these seuē: paper, incke, pen, penknife, ruler, deske, and dustbox, of these the three first are most necessarie, the foure latter very requisite.

Choyse of paper.
The whitest, finest, and smothest paper is best.

To make inke.
Put into a quart of water two ounces of right gumme Arabick, fiue ounces of galles, and three of copras. Let it stād couered in the warme sunne, and so will it the sooner proue good incke. To boyle the sayd stuffe together a little vpon the fire would make it more speedy for your writyng: but þ vnboyled yeldeth a fayrer glosse, ē lōger indureth. In stead of water wine were best for this purpose. Refresh your inke with wine, or vineger, whē it wareth thicke,

This is a page from Francis Clement's book on writing. It is printed, like the horn book, in the **secretary** *hand – the style of handwriting which most ordinary schoolchildren learnt.*

1 What equipment does Clement say a writer ought to have? What do you think a penknife and a dustbox were used for?

2 Write down five words that by our modern standards are spelt wrongly.

3 Clement has spelt one rather important word in two different ways. See if you can find the two versions and then write them down with the proper modern spelling alongside.

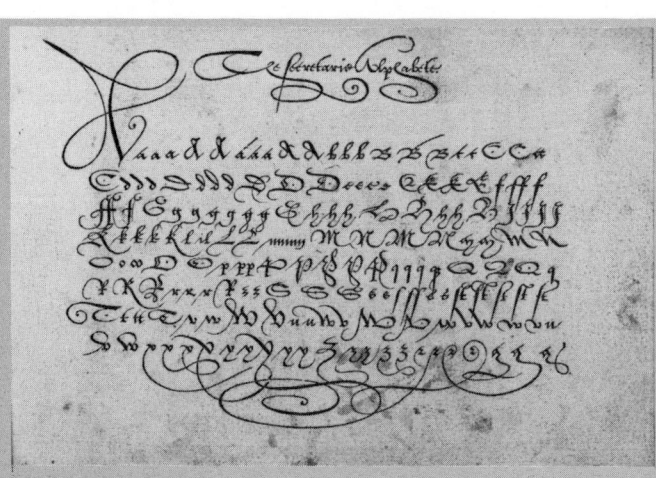

This is the quicker version of the secretary hand. An expert of the time described it 'as the only usual hand of England for dispatching of all manner of business'.

*Henry VIII's three children – and others – were now beginning to learn the beautiful **Italic** style seen in this illustration. Within a hundred years this style was to take over completely from the secretary hand.*

1 What else is written on the horn book (besides the Lord's Prayer) which shows how important religious teaching was to the Tudors?

2 Make your own sheet for a horn book. Use A4 paper, and write the letters either in modern script or in one of those illustrated here. The Lord's Prayer may be omitted if necessary.

3 Imagine yourself as a Tudor pupil, and make words out of ten of the combination groups on the horn book, i.e. ab: able.

4 If there had been room on the horn book, what do you think would have been the next row of combination letters?

5 Look closely at the example of Italic hand.

a) Which letters in our modern alphabet seem to be missing from this one?

b) In those days the letter S could be written in two different ways. The modern method is used several times in this piece of writing. Find an example of the old method and copy down the word in which it appears. Can you think of a reason why this old method was eventually dropped?

c) On one occasion the writer has found that he has not given himself enough room to finish a word. See if you can find the word, and explain, or draw, what he has done to get out of the difficulty.

The education ladder

Before they were old enough to attend a grammar school, boys (and sometimes girls) went to a 'petties' school. The name comes from the French word *petit*: small. At Walter's petties school an elderly woman taught him to read and write from a horn book. She was not a very good teacher because the best scholars would not take on this kind of work. One Tudor schoolmaster said that these teachers were sometimes 'poor women . . . whose necessities compel them to undertake it as a mere shelter from beggary'. In other words, they must teach or starve! And the author of an early writing-book, Francis Clement, said that children:

> almost everywhere are first taught either in private by men or women altogether *rude* and utterly ignorant of the due composing and *just* spelling of words: or else in common schools, most commonly by boys, very seldom or never by any of sufficient skill. . . . How few be there under the age of seven or eight years that are *towardly abled or praisably furnished for* reading? And as many there be above those years that can neither readily spell or rightly write even the common words of our English.

uneducated; correct

properly trained

But Francis Clement knows what should be done: if they use *his* writing-book matters will improve 'within a month'!

1 Who else besides men and women used to teach the pupils at 'petties' level, according to Francis Clement?

2 Look at the picture of a school on page 4:
   a) Is there any evidence that at least *one* other subject besides Latin was taught?
   b) Is there any evidence that some of the boys are still at the 'petties' level of learning?

3 Imagine yourself in the classroom on page 4 and invent the incident that might have led to the beating.

Find as much writing equipment as you can in this schoolroom. Are these boys 'petties'?

At long last Walter heard the clock strike eleven. All the morning he had been working away at his grammar book, translating into English a seemingly endless list of rules of behaviour, all written in Latin. He thought that he had quite enough of this at home, for his parents often lectured him about manners out of their *Boke of Nurture, or Schoole of good maners*. Here are some of the rules:

   Get up in good time
   Make your bed neatly
   Say your prayers
   Clean your shoes
   Brush your clothes
   Comb your hair
   Wash your hands and face
   Don't pare your nails at table
   Don't pick your teeth with a knife
   Don't drink your soup too loudly and don't blow on it to cool it
   Don't cram your mouth or plate too full
   Don't lean your elbows on the table or stare about
   Eat what is put before you.

'Well,' thought Walter, 'I wish I *could* eat what's put before me. If old Carey doesn't let us go soon the dinner will be all spoilt.' But just at that moment the schoolmaster spoke: 'You have worked well this week, and have been obedient and have made good progress. So you may have this afternoon free for your pleasure and recreation.' Some murmurs of joy started up at these words but soon stopped when Carey's hand moved towards the handle of the birch.

'Remember,' he continued, 'what I always tell you: on your way home raise your caps to people you know, don't run in heaps like a swarm of bees, and don't whoop and shout in the streets. Now, we shall have our prayer and recite two verses of Psalm 23, but first let me remind you of what St Paul said in his epistle to the Ephesians: "Children, obey your parents in the Lord: for this is right."'

1 If you were drawing up rules of behaviour for your children nowadays which of those on this page would you keep and what others would you add, if any?

2 If Master Carey had not let them have the afternoon off, they would have started work again at 1 p.m. and finished at about 5.
   a) In this particular school how much time was spent in the classroom daily?
   b) How long was the dinner break?
   c) How do these hours compare with those at your school?

Grammar schools such as the one Walter attended, were so called originally because they were schools where Latin grammar was taught. At school Walter might have found Latin boring, but in a future career it could prove very valuable. Latin would be essential if he wanted to take up a profession in medicine, the law, or the Church, and it was also used all over Europe as a common method of communication with people of another language. So it would be very useful in the business and political world abroad.

The method of teaching Latin to beginners was for the boys to learn passages off by heart and to use the language in ordinary, everyday conversation. In some schools they would be punished if they spoke English! Later they studied the rules of Latin grammar and read books by famous Roman writers.

Other school subjects were considered much less important than Latin; but Walter might possibly study some English literature and learn some arithmetic and geography. Religious education had a regular place in the timetable and boys were expected to learn off by heart the Ten Commandments, the Lord's Prayer, and other religious passages.

In many towns in Tudor England there were schools with free places for poorer children whose parents would not otherwise have been able to send them to school. Richer parents paid fees according to their rank in life. For example, at Shrewsbury school, founded in 1552, there was free education for all, but admission fees were charged as follows:

- A lord's son   10 shillings
- A knight's son   6 shillings and 8 pence
- A gentleman's son   3 shillings and 4 pence
- A citizen's son   4 pence.

Thomas Heron was a schoolboy who died aged 14 in 1517. This picture is on his tomb. Some schoolboys wore a long gown like this one. How does he carry his pen case and ink pot?

This is a photograph of the schoolroom in the grammar school at Stratford-on-Avon. William Shakespeare was a pupil here, and the room has not changed much since his day.

University could be the next stage if Walter did well at grammar school. He would probably go at the age of 15; sixteenth-century 'scholars', as they were called, were usually younger than modern students. There were only two English universities then, Oxford and Cambridge. There he would study Latin grammar, Logic (the science of reasoning correctly), Rhetoric (the art of speaking or writing well), Arithmetic, Geometry, Musical theory, and Astronomy (study of the stars).

Even though they had left school, scholars still had to obey a great many strict rules. For example: students were not allowed into inns, tobacco shops, theatres, cock-fights or bear-baitings. They could be punished for wearing silks or satins, or ruffs that were too large; for wearing their hair too long, for not attending church, and for keeping hawks, guns or dogs. And a student could be beaten if he:

> prevented his fellows from studying or sleeping by singing, making a noise, shouting, or discharging guns, or by making any other kind of uproar or din.

It is important to remember however that many ordinary children, especially in the country, never went to school at all – let alone university.

Work at home

At home, Kate's mother, Alice, was busier than usual. Her husband, John Procter, was an important glovemaker in the town and would expect everything to be particularly well prepared for Master Carey's visit. Meg, the maidservant, was doing the dusting and then making sure the cooking fire was burning well; the *pewter* [a mixture of tin and lead] plates and steel knives had to be scoured, the napkins folded neatly, the cloth laid, and the chair and stools set ready.

The Procters were the proud owners of two silver plates and these had to be given a good polish so that they might look their best displayed on the cupboard. But their most prized possession was a silver-gilt 'salt' and Mistress Alice was seeing to the cleaning of this herself – she did not trust anyone else.

Another luxury was a set of 'Venice glasses'. These came from Italy and replaced the pewter drinking cups on special occasions. Meg was sent to fetch a flagon of wine from the nearby inn because ale would not be considered good enough today.

Now the food was prepared. The meal was to start with oysters, so pepper and vinegar had to be placed ready on the table. The loaves had to be inspected for burnt crusts which must be chipped off before the bread was cut into slices and put by each place on the table.

The leg of mutton, stuffed with garlic, had to be well basted with fat as it turned on the spit, and the turnips, cabbage and onions had to be put in the pot to boil. Meg fetched the cold venison pasty from the store cupboard and started to arrange on plates the dessert of jellies, apricots, quince pie and almond tart.

A Tudor kitchen.

Although people in Tudor England usually kept most of their belongings in chests, cupboards were sometimes used to display plates and dishes.

1 In the picture of a kitchen find the adjustable hook from which the cooking pot is hanging.
Draw a diagram to illustrate the way this hook works.

2 The servant in the foreground is placing a chicken on a spit. At one end of the spit there is a circular disc. See if you can work out what is the purpose of this disc and draw a sketch to explain how it is used.

3 a) What is the woman in front of the fire doing?
b) What is the purpose of the two long pans under the spit by the fire?

Salt-cellars and trenchers

It does not seem particularly important to us today to have a grand salt-cellar, but in Tudor times food so often lacked freshness or taste that salt was essential to make it more interesting. In larger houses, too, there was an old custom that the salt-cellar's position on the table marked the dividing line between where the grand and the less grand people sat.

A good host obviously did not want people dipping their food directly into the splendid salt-cellar and so very often a guest would be provided with a

A very elegant salt-cellar made of silver. The Procter family would have been unlikely to afford one as grand as this.

Salt-cellars came in many different designs. This is another one which might be used in a rich household.

wooden **trencher**. This was a rectangular or square board in the middle of which was a hollowed-out circle, roughly 13–15 cm across, in which you put your meat and gravy. At one corner of the trencher was a smaller hollow in which you had your own supply of salt. This is what is being referred to in a manual of instruction for the young called *The Babees Book*. It says:

> Do not touch the salt in the salt-cellar with any meat, but lay salt honestly on your trencher for that is *courtesy* [good manners].

■ Draw a picture of your own grand salt-cellar.

Mistress Procter might have owned decorated wooden trenchers like these.

Servants were often treated more like friends of the family than people to be looked down on or ignored. They were frequently taken into service when they were children and they shared the fortunes and misfortunes of their employers. But just as the children of the household were liable to be beaten, so the servants too might expect the rod if they did something wrong. They might be fined, too. Here is a list of fines drawn up by Sir John Harington in 1592:

Absence from morning or evening prayers	twopence
Swearing	penny an oath
Bed still unmade after 8 a.m.	penny
Breaking a glass	cost deducted from wages
Dinner late	cook fined sixpence
Failure to change shirt on Sunday or replace missing buttons on doublet	penny
Flirting with the maids	fourpence.

But a hard-working maidservant could learn a great deal from her mistress about how to run a household, and if she married she could look forward to receiving a generous wedding present from her employers.

1 How can you tell that Sir John Harington employed boy as well as girl servants?

2 Make up some extra offences and fines which Sir John might have added to his list.

3 Use the information in this section 'Work at home' to plan a timetable for Mistress Procter's only servant, Meg, on the day that Master Carey came to dinner.

Education for girls

Girls were much more likely than boys to be taught at home, especially if they came from ordinary families, although there were a few girls' schools. For instance, as you will see later, there must have been some schooling in Norwich for very poor children including girls. But most poor children just learnt what they could as they helped their parents in the house and out in the fields. Even four- and five-year-olds worked hard to help keep the family. All would have helped with hedge trimming, ditch cleaning and collecting acorns and beechnuts for the pigs, and they could have done useful work in haymaking and harvest time.

Here are some of the domestic jobs which a girl would learn from her mother: herb collecting (for cooking and medicine); salting meat; care of poultry; baking and brewing; butter and cheese making; soap making; spinning and weaving; fruit and nut collecting; feather collecting (for stuffing pillows etc.).

A servant girl doing the dusting.

The main aim of a girl's upbringing in Tudor times was to make her suitable for marriage. Besides the skills mentioned above she would also be taught reading and writing, and possibly enough arithmetic to help her keep household accounts. She would spend a lot of time learning needlework, or 'pricking of clouts' as it was then called. She would practise all the different stitches by making a 'sampler'. This was a piece of cloth on which she would embroider verses from the Bible, the letters of the alphabet, her name, and anything else she fancied.

A girl might get the chance to go and live with another family when she was 12 or 13 – perhaps a wealthier family than her own if her parents could arrange it. There she could learn more about running a household, and a suitable marriage might be arranged for her.

A sampler made for Alice Lee in 1598. Notice that it even mentions the time of day she was born! Draw your own plan for your own sampler using some of the patterns from the embroidery.

13

Walter scrambled off his bench and was away down the street in a moment, but Master Carey felt he had to appear more dignified than his pupils, so, after locking the school door, he strolled in a stately manner towards the Procters' house, his black gown, velvet hat and tall cane showing the world how important he was. It was a pity that a woman happened to empty a chamber-pot out of an upstairs window just as he was passing underneath, but luckily he was able to dodge out of the way, although he almost stepped straight into the open drain that ran down the centre of the street.

Streets in Tudor towns could be very dirty. Piles of manure would often be left lying around, encouraging rats and disease. The smells were very unpleasant, especially in the height of summer.

Mistress Procter ushered him to the table and as he was an important guest the carved oak chair was reserved for him; the rest of the family sat on benches or stools. Kate made a curtsey to the guest, and Walter, who had been washing his hands and face in the kitchen, rushed in to give a hurried bow and say grace. Meg brought in the oysters, and the apprentice, Richard, stood by with a basin of water and a towel, for with spoons and knives only and no forks, hands soon got greasy.

'Well, Mistress,' said Master Carey, 'I see you serve good, honest English food, no foreign nonsense. I heard tell recently of a man who was sent a present of a barrel of caviare by a great lady. He tasted it and sent back the message, "Commend me to my good Lady and thank her honour, and tell her we have black soap enough already."'

The conversation then turned to other expensive delicacies from abroad, for example sugar, turkeys and drinking chocolate; but after a while Mistress Procter noticed that Walter was getting restless and gave him permission to leave the table. After a polite bow to Master Carey he was away to join his friends for a swim down at the river.

After his swim there would be a wide choice of games for him to play, many of them the same as those played today.

1 Look at the cover picture and note down eight games or activities that might still be played nowadays.

2 About half-way up the picture on the right-hand edge there is a boy holding a stick in the air dangling something from it. Invent a set of rules for this game.

Games and entertainments

Football was popular, although it was a more dangerous game in Tudor times than it is now. There were no rules and no referee, and any number of people could take part. The goals might be three miles apart and the game could go on all day. Often apprentices played it in the streets and shopkeepers boarded up their shops to protect their goods. This is what a writer of the time said about the game. It is, he writes:

> a bloody and murdering practice.... Doth not everyone lie in wait for his *adversary* [opponent], seeking to overthrow him, and to pitch him on the nose, though it be upon hard stones ... so he have him down? ... so that by this means sometimes their necks are broken, sometimes their backs, sometimes their legs, sometimes their arms; ... sometime their noses gush out with blood, sometime their eyes start out.

It is not surprising that football was banned in Tudor times in some towns, including London.

Other outdoor games that Walter would have the chance of playing were:

Kayles like nine-pins (see picture). If you aimed at the pins with a stick it was called 'club kayles'.

Stool-ball ancestor of modern cricket. The stool acted as a wicket and you hit the ball either with a piece of wood or with your fist ('bare-knuckle stool-ball').

Wrestling, **quoit throwing**, **archery**, **leaping and running**, **prisoner's base**, **throwing the sledge** (hammer), **fives** (played against a church wall), **bandy-ball** (early form of golf or hockey), **bowls**, **fishing**, **pall-mall** (a game in which a ball was driven through an iron ring). These last three sports were also enjoyed by women and girls.

A sheep's bladder was often used for a football though it was more likely to be stuffed with rags than to be blown up with this rather modern looking kind of pump.

Kayles.

You will see from this picture that football was not the only game that could be played in the street. What do you think these apprentices are playing?

One day Queen Elizabeth looked out of her window and saw this:

> About 3 of the clock, ten of the Earl of Hertford's servants all Somersetshire men, in a square green court, before her Majesty's window, did hang up lines, squaring out the form of a tennis-court making a cross line in the middle. In this square they (being stripped of their doublets) played five to five, with the hand-ball, at bord and cord (as they term it) to the great liking of her Highness.

What modern game does this remind you of?

Nine Men's Morris

One popular game in Tudor times was 'Nine Men's Morris'. This was a board game, but it could be played in the open air if you scratched lines on the ground and made small holes at every angle. Shakespeare refers to the open-air game in his play *A Midsummer Night's Dream* where one of the characters says: 'The Nine Men's Morris is filled up with mud.'

■ Make your own board by copying the diagram in the margin onto a sheet of A4 paper (or larger). The game is for two players, each of whom has nine men of contrasting colours. You could use draughts pieces, coins or buttons.

Nine Men's Morris.

Rules: Each player in turn places a piece on one of the circles. The aim is to get three of your men in a straight row (as in noughts-and-crosses) and also to prevent your opponent doing so. Whenever you make such a row you are allowed to remove one of your opponent's pieces as long as it is not one of a row of three. When all the pieces have been played, the players, still keeping in turn, move their pieces along the lines from circle to circle, one circle at a time, still trying to form lines of three. The first to remove all his opponent's pieces is the winner. Other indoor games were:

Cards The court cards in the modern pack are still shown wearing Tudor dress. Card games were very popular and many children particularly enjoyed 'Trump': in this game, before you started to play you decided which card was to be 'trump'. Each player then took turns to put down a card face up on the table and when the 'trump' card appeared everyone had to thump the table with his left hand and shout, 'Trump!' The last to hit the table was the loser of that round and had to pay a forfeit.

■ In what way is this game different from the modern game of 'Snap'?

Popular board games were **draughts**, **backgammon**, **slide-thrift** (shove ha'penny) – and adults and children enjoyed **chess**.

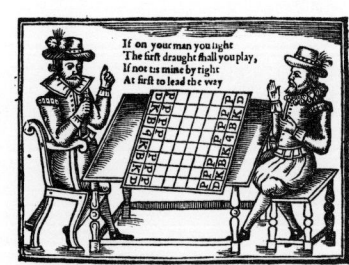

One of these men is saying to the other: 'If you choose your colour from these two hidden pieces, then you play first; otherwise I do'.

1 Which man is speaking?

2 What evidence is there in the picture in the margin that these are probably wealthy men?

16

After their dinner, John Procter and his guest decided they would like to stroll down to the beargarden. Walter joined them there and as his father was feeling in a generous mood after his good dinner, he treated them all to a seat in the stands. Before the baiting started the audience was entertained by a showman and his performing horse.

'Well, Master John,' said the schoolmaster, 'what sport shall we see this afternoon, do you think?'

'Plenty, I shouldn't wonder, if that famous bear Harry Hunks is to appear,' replied Procter; 'They say he killed two dogs with one blow last week.'

This performing horse was trained to tell the audience which number turned up on the dice, by tapping the ground with his hoof.

'That must have been a grand sight,' answered Carey. 'But when I was a boy of Walter's age, back in King Henry's time, I remember seeing a bear-baiting in the water! My father and I were staying in London and we were told that if we wanted to catch a glimpse of the King we must hurry down to the river. So we did – and there he was in his royal barge with a number of other boats around him, and they were baiting bears in the water, poking at them with great sticks and shouting and yelling. And then one of the bears broke loose and scrambled into a boat that happened to be passing by and the boat began to sink and the boatman fell into the river. Then the King must have thought that things were getting too dangerous because he shouted: "Away, away with the bear, and let us all go hence!"'

As Master Carey finished speaking the first bear was being brought in and the show began.

Here a German visitor to Tudor England described a bull- and bear-baiting that he witnessed:

> the bulls and bears ... are fastened behind, and then worried by great English bulldogs but not without great risk to the dogs, from the horns of the one and the teeth of the other; and it sometimes happens that they are killed upon the spot; fresh ones are immediately supplied in the place of those that are wounded or tired. To this entertainment there often follows that of whipping a blinded bear, which is performed by 5 or 6 men, standing circularly with whips ... he defends himself with all his force and skill, vigorously throwing down all who come within his reach ... tearing the whips out of their hands and breaking them.

People in Tudor times did not feel as we do today about cruelty to animals. Queen Elizabeth herself took pleasure in attending bear-baiting and would invite her foreign visitors to watch it. Cock-fighting was also popular. The cocks were trained for fighting and had metal spurs fastened to their feet to make their attacks on each other more vicious. On Shrove Tuesday every year schoolboys were encouraged to bring their own fighting cocks to school to compete against others. Even more unpleasant, perhaps, was the 'sport' of burying a cock up to the neck in sand and then stoning it to death.

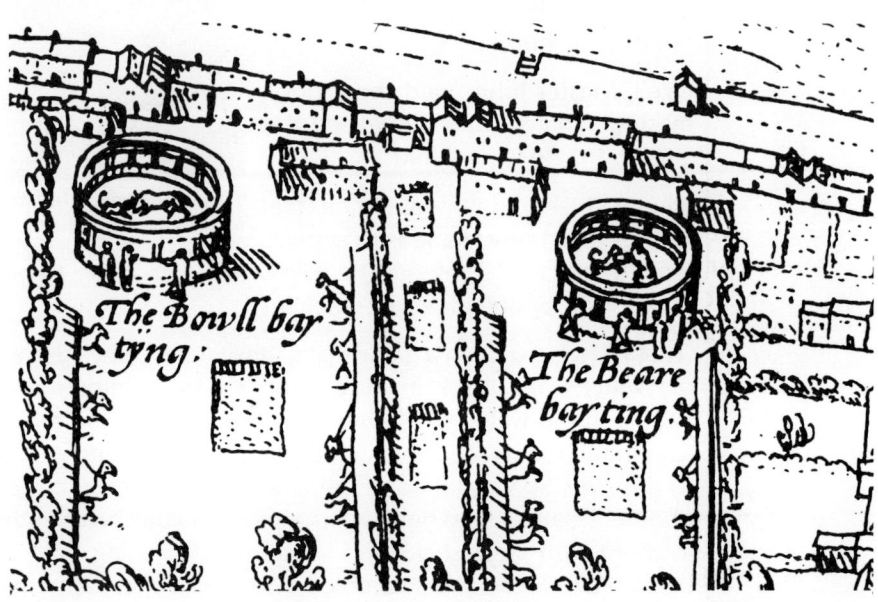

These are the bull- and bear-baiting rings on the south bank of the Thames at London. In 1590, we are told, three bulls, five bears, and 100 dogs were kept at the Beargarden. At the end of the show there was a firework display.

Not everybody approved, however, of such entertainments. One writer of the time said that bear-baiting was:

> a filthy, stinking and loathsome game.... What Christian heart can take pleasure to see one poor beast to rend, tear and kill another, and all for his foolish pleasure?

Thursday was usually the day when bear- and bull-baiting took place; on the other days the Procters could have gone to the theatre. Here they would have seen plays of all sorts from comedies to tragedies, and there would be plenty of 'special effects' to please the blood-thirsty. For example, in a play called *Battle of Alcazar* the stage directions for a scene where three characters are killed state that you will need '3 *vials* [little flasks] of blood and a sheep's *gather* [heart, liver and lungs of an animal]'.

The actors must have hidden these props under their doublets and were then 'slaughtered' in a very gory and messy way as the blood and guts came spilling out!

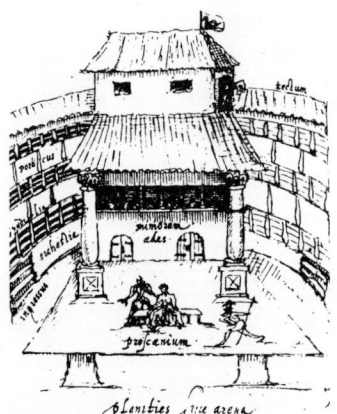

A contemporary drawing of a Tudor theatre. Try to find out more about what performances were like. Where do you think the play took place, and the audience sat or stood?

Kate and her mother always enjoyed a good laugh at the comedy *Gammer Gurton's Needle*, in which a housewife loses her needle while mending her husband's breeches. Everyone is suspected of stealing the needle until her husband finds it – painfully and unexpectedly – by sitting on it!

Although women and girls enjoyed going to the theatre in Tudor times, it was not considered respectable for them to act. So women's parts in plays were taken by boys. That is why Shakespeare often made his heroines disguise themselves as boys, because then the boy actors would find it easier to act naturally. It looks as if he disapproved of boy actors, though other dramatists wrote plays specially for them. A character in one of his plays compares them to a nest full of squawking baby birds with their mouths gaping wide open!

Being an actor was not an easy life for a boy. Plays changed very frequently, so there was a huge number of lines to learn by heart; and when his voice broke he would be out of a job, unless he had proved himself so good an actor that he was kept on as an adult.

Queen Elizabeth was particularly fond of watching plays, and so her choir boys from the Chapel Royal were specially trained to act as well as to sing. They lived together in a boarding school in Blackfriars which had its own private theatre; but it was not acting practice all the time – they also had to do ordinary lessons, and singing, music and dancing.

Arden of Feversham was a popular and thrilling play about ordinary people, not about kings and lords. The story was based on a real murder case when Arden's wife and her lover (a tailor) hired two professional thugs, Shakbag and Black Will, to murder her husband. But the crime was discovered and Mrs Arden and her lover were executed.
Who are all the people in this picture?
What game was Arden playing just before he was murdered?

Babies and toddlers

> After clearing the dinner, Kate and her mother did not want to join the others at the bear-baiting. They had a special visit to make. There was a new baby next door, and they were going to the christening party.

In this picture we can see two babies firmly wrapped up in their swaddling clothes, which are richly covered with silk brocade.

A double portrait like this is unusual but the twin mothers wanted to celebrate the occasion in a special way. They themselves were not only born on the same day, but were married on the same day, and they had their babies on the same day!

1 Are the mothers and babies dressed identically?

2 How much evidence can you find that this is not a poor family?

Women friends and relations always helped as much as they could when a baby was born. Midwives looked after the mother and baby during the birth. There were strict regulations about how they should behave. Cleanliness was very important. They must keep their nails clean and well cut, and before starting work must smear their hands with butter and remove all rings and bracelets. They must be careful not to pass on gossip that they may hear in the houses they visit. An instruction book of the time says that the midwife must not be a 'blabber, or reporter of any thing she shall either hear or see in secret in the house or person of her she hath delivered'. The instructions also say that the midwife must have in readiness:

bonnets
nappies
low stools for midwives to sit on when helping to deliver babies

soap, candles, beds, shirts, *biggins*, waistcoats, headbands, *swaddle-bands*, *cross-clothes*, bibs, *tail clouts*, mantles, hose, shoes, coats, petticoats, cradle and *crickets*.

The cross-cloth was to tie around the mother's forehead to stop her getting unattractive wrinkles.

As soon as the baby was born its body was rubbed with oil of acorns to protect it against smoke and cold. It was then washed in warm water. The midwife now swaddled the baby, that is to say she used the swaddle-bands mentioned above, which were like long bandages, to wrap the baby up like a parcel so that it could not move its limbs. The purpose of this was to protect it from draughts, to prevent it scratching itself and to stop it going on all fours like an animal! It was also supposed to ensure that its limbs grew straight.

A book of 1540 says:

> the nurse must ... bind every part right and in his due place and order ... and not crookedly; ... for in this it is as it is in young and tender ... plants and twigs, the which even as you bow them in their youth, so will they evermore remain unto age. And even so the infant if it be bound and swaddled, the *members* lying right and straight, then shall it grow straight and upright.   limbs

Although midwives made efforts to be hygienic, childbirth was a risky business. Visitors crowded in to cheer and comfort the mother, and sanitation was primitive.

1 Make labelled drawings of the equipment of a Tudor midwife. Group all the baby's clothes together, and draw in a separate box the clothes a modern newborn baby is likely to wear. Why are modern baby clothes so different?

2 Look at the picture on this page. Describe what all the people in the picture are doing.
What evidence can you see to show that the health of the mother and baby was at risk?

Looking after a mother and her newborn baby.

21

A sixteenth-century picture shows Death seizing a baby from a villager's family.

Women expected childbirth to be difficult and dangerous, and as medical knowledge was very limited many mothers and babies died. Sometimes 'cures' were little more than the midwife's spells and charms. A modern mother would not have much confidence in this prescription for increasing her milk: 'take the powder of earth-worms dried and drunken in the broth of a *neat's* [cow's] tongue.'

It has been calculated that in Tudor England one out of every 40 pregnant women died in childbirth. Compare this with the figures for nowadays which are one out of 10 000!

The death-rate among babies was also high. The parish registers in the second half of the sixteenth century, which record births and deaths, suggest that one in seven babies died in the first year of their lives. This figure became worse in certain areas: in one of the poorer London parishes, for instance, the death-rate rose to about one in three. Another bad area for children's deaths was the low-lying, marshy Fen districts in East Anglia.

After the first year the child had a better chance of surviving: approximately one in 14 died between the ages of one and four, and one in 33 between five and nine.

1 Give some reasons why the death-rate in towns would be higher than in the country.

2 Why do you think the death-rate was particularly high in the Fens?

3 Children did not die only of disease. Think of dangers arising from open fires, cooking, animals, ponds, etc. Look at the picture in the margin and at the picture on page 21.
   a) Make a list of the accidents which might happen to a Tudor toddler and say why they would be less likely to happen to a modern child.
   b) What dangers does a modern child face that a Tudor child would not meet?

Feeding the baby

There were no specially prepared baby foods in Tudor times. Infants were kept on their mother's milk – or the milk of foster-mothers (called wet-nurses) – well into their second year. After that they were given cow's milk or 'pap', a mixture of bread and milk. They moved on to adult food as soon as they had enough teeth to cope with it; but they were discouraged from eating fruit, which was supposed to give them the 'flux' or diarrhoea.

When the Princess Elizabeth was three years old, the Steward in charge of her household wanted her to have meals with the adults; but her nurse objected:

suitable
different kinds of

It is not *meet* for the child of her age to keep such rule yet. If she do, I dare not take it upon me to keep her Grace in health; for there she shall see *divers* meats, and fruits, and wine, which it would be hard for me to restrain her Grace from.

Christenings

Babies were baptised as soon as possible, because the Church taught that a child who died unchristened would not go to Heaven. The mother was not usually fit enough to come to the church so soon, so the child's godparents would take her place. The godparents, in fact, often chose the child's name, usually calling the baby after themselves. On one occasion, in 1568, two godfathers almost had a fight in the church about the right name for their godson. The clergyman stopped the quarrel by choosing the name himself. Because the child had been born on St Paul's Day, the clergyman named him Paul – although the baby already had a brother with the same name!

1 Look at the family tree on page 48, and check how many of the names in the margin were also the names of Tudor kings and queens. Try to find out which of the other names belonged to earlier kings and queens.

2 How many, if any, of the people in your form have the same name as any of the present Royal family?

3 Nowadays, what kinds of famous people are children named after, besides members of the Royal family?

Common names of the time.
Girls: Mary, Alice, Elizabeth, Anne, Margaret, Katherine
Boys: Henry, Edward, William, John, Richard, Robert, Thomas

After the christening ceremony the baby was wrapped in a special white linen cloth called a 'chrisom' before it was carried home again. The white stood for innocence, and the baby wore the chrisom for about a month afterwards. If it died during that period it was buried in it.

After the christening there was a party, and friends and relations gave presents just as they do today. Among the more wealthy a suitable present would be a set of 'apostle' spoons (spoons with the figures of the 12 apostles on the handles) or a teething ring made of coral set in a silver mount. Poorer people would offer a small sum of money or possibly an article of clothing.

■ Describe the visit by Kate Procter and her mother to the christening party of their neighbour's baby.

This is a pewter porringer or bowl for eating porridge out of. It would be a typical christening present.

Children's clothes

Portraits are the best evidence we have for children's clothes in Tudor times. But there are two difficulties when we try to work out what children like Kate and Walter wore. The first difficulty is one we have already met: only rich people could afford to have their portraits painted. No record like that would have been left by poorer children. Secondly, portraits certainly give us a lot of information about what people wore as their best clothes – but even rich children may have had ordinary clothes for everyday use. We just don't know. However, we can be sure that clothes were always a great deal more elaborate than now; and rich children's clothes give us an idea of what more ordinary children wore, although the materials would have been less expensive.

Boys dressed like their fathers, but not until they were six or seven. Up to that age they wore more or less the same as girls, as you can see from the portrait of Sir John Thynne's son below. (Look also at the boy with a sword in the picture on page 50.) You can tell the difference between the gowns for boys and girls: boys gowns have buttons down the front.

Sir John Thynne's son aged six months.

Lady Arbella Stuart aged 23 months.

The future King James I of England aged eight.

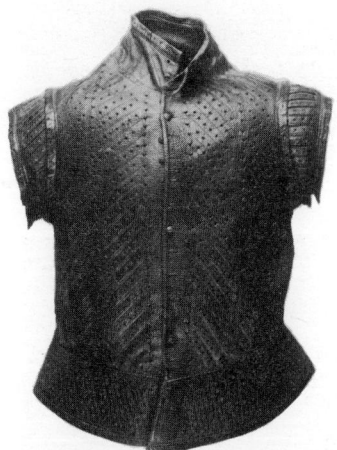

A sixteenth-century boy's leather doublet which you can still see in the Museum of London.

At seven, a child's second teeth often begin to appear, and in Tudor times it was thought that at this age a boy could start to tell right from wrong and become capable of sin and crime. So it was a turning point in his life, and a suitable time for 'breeching' or changing over to men's clothes – **breeches**, **doublet** (jacket), and **hose** (long stockings like tights). Sometimes the doublet was 'slashed' – slits were cut in its fabric so that tufts of the shirt underneath could be pulled through to make a contrast of colours.

A boy at a sixteenth-century boarding school tells us how he got dressed:

> After waking up, I got out of bed, I put on my doublet.... I sat on a stool, I took my breeches and stockings and pulled both on, I took my shoes, I fastened my breeches to my doublet with laces, I tied my stockings with garters above the knee, I took my belt, I combed my hair, I took my cap which I arranged carefully, I put on my robe, and then I left the bedroom.

You will notice that over the rest of his clothes he puts on a robe; this was like a long coat, and was sometimes worn by school boys.

After growing out of her baby clothes, a girl would straight away wear a smaller version of her mother's dress. So, when getting dressed, she had to put on:

Smock: a loose-fitting long garment made of linen or flannel.

Stockings: usually knitted and made of wool, though for the wealthy silk was becoming fashionable.

Ribbons: to secure the stockings just above or below the knee.

Bodice: this was separate from the skirt, and to give the fashionable rigid look it was usually stiffened with thin lengths of wood or whalebone.

Sleeves: your mother had to help you with these because they were put on separately and were tied or pinned to the bodice. The join was hidden by 'wings'. (Can you find any in the picture on page 50?)

Several **waist-petticoats**.

Finally a skirt or **kirtle**: this was split in front to show the top petticoat underneath, which would be finely decorated. As you grew older, you wore under your skirts one of the fashionable foundations. At its simplest this would be a padded roll around the waist (the common name for it was a bum-roll!). This made your skirts fall straight to the ground. More elaborate were the various 'farthingales', stiffened with cane, which made the skirts stick out, sometimes 60 cm or more (see the older girl at the bottom of this page and the girls on page 50. Also, can you see the farthingale on page 28?).

Two little girls aged four and five, painted in 1590.

1 Who would be the quickest to dress, boys or girls? Who needed the most help?

2 In Tudor times do you think it was easier for boys to be more active than girls? Give reasons.

3 Write down some activities which you usually enjoy, but which would be difficult if you wore Tudor clothes.

4 Use the pictures in this section and the picture of the Cobham family on page 2. Check the ages of the girls, and the dates the pictures were painted. List the names and ages of all the girls, and choose one to sketch.

5 What differences can you see between the Cobham girls and the 12-year-old on this page? What is the reason for these differences?

6 This book began with Walter Procter getting dressed. Imagine you are Kate Procter getting dressed at the beginning of the same day. Describe what happens (remember you may need some help – and it is a busy morning).
Use the list on this page, and the pictures, to illustrate your description.

A girl of about 12 or 13, also painted in about 1590.

Nursery rhymes, fairy tales, riddles and toys

Tudor children knew many of the **nursery rhymes** which are still popular today, though perhaps with slightly different words. For example: *Who killed Cock Robin, Ride a cock-horse, Little Boy Blue, Sing a song of sixpence, Old King Cole, Three Blind Mice,* and *A Frog he would a-wooing go* (see music below).

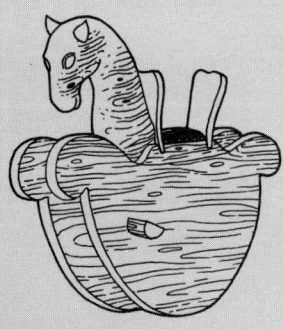

What do you think is the modern version of this rhyme?

Jack boy, ho boy news
   the cat is in the well,
let us ring now for her *knell* [funeral bell],
   ding dong ding dong bell.

Here is a nursery rhyme that was popular with the Tudors but is forgotten today:

Tom-a-lin and his wife, and his wife's mother
They went over a bridge all three together
The bridge was broken, and they fell in,
'The devil go with all,' quoth Tom-a-lin.

This music is dated 1611, just a few years after the death of Queen Elizabeth I. The second verse goes like this:

The frog would a wooing ride,
   humble dum, humble dum,
Sword and buckler [shield] by his side
   Tweedle, tweedle twino.

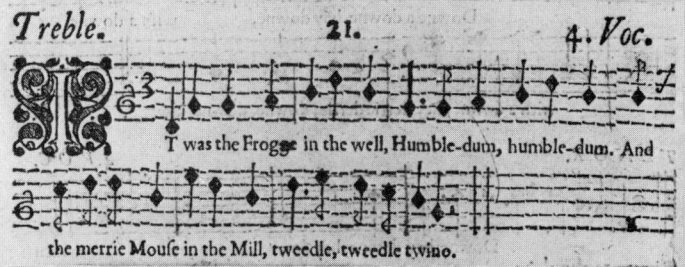

■ A modern writer has calculated that one in four of all nursery rhymes known to us today were known, in some form or another, to the Tudors as well. Why have nursery rhymes lasted so well?

Some **fairy stories** Tudor children would have known: Tom Thumb, Babes in the Wood, Jack the Giant Killer, Beauty and the Beast.

■ In these Tudor **riddles** the wrong answers have been placed opposite the questions. Write down A, B, C, D for the questions and opposite each letter write the number of the correct answer.

  A. What carried the best burden that ever was borne?   1. The Earth.
  B. Who was Adam's mother?   2. The ass that carried our Lady, when she fled with our Lord into Egypt.
  C. Who killed one fourth part of all the people in the world?   3. Smoke.
  D. A house full, a yard full, and you cannot catch a bowl full. What is it?
  4. Cain when he killed Abel.

Answer no. 4 is in the Bible (Genesis, chapter 4) – no problem to a Tudor child.

How many of these riddles show how keen the Tudors were on religious education?

How do you think a modern child might answer question C?

Apprentices and others

Richard Greene, the apprentice, was left behind to look after John Procter's glove shop when everyone else went out. He was 12 years old and had been a glovemaker's apprentice since he was ten. This had been arranged very carefully between his father and John Procter.

INDENTURE (agreement)

'Richard Greene binds himself apprentice to John Procter...'

John Procter's promises
He would keep Richard seven years
He would train him in glovemaking
He would provide food, drink and lodging in his own house
He would provide Richard with stockings and shoes.

Richard Greene's promises
He paid £10
He would obey his master
He would not steal
He would not gamble
He would not buy or sell except for his master
He would not give away trade secrets.

■ Make your own 'old' document showing the indenture between Richard Greene and John Procter.

Richard did not spend all his time in the workshop learning how to make gloves. It was his job also to take down the shutters in the morning, open up the shop, and get everything clean and ready for the day's work. Then he had to go to the conduit to fetch water for the household, bringing it back in a big bucket.

By the time he returned the streets were filling up with people and his master sent him out again to attract customers into the shop by shouting: 'Fine gloves for sale, fine gloves for sale! What do you lack, sirs? Fine gloves for sale!'

He was competing with apprentices in other trades and with the street-sellers too, so there was a great deal of noise.

A master and his two apprentices in a tailoring shop. A farthingale hangs on the wall.

Rules for apprentices

A master punished his apprentice if he did wrong, just as he punished his own children – that is, with a box on the ear or a whipping. But he also tried to see that the boy kept out of trouble in the streets, and he gave him religious instruction. For example, in one of the churches in York there were special seats reserved for families and apprentices

> to the intent that the . . . master might [over]see the *conversation* [behaviour] of the said apprentices.

In this way the master was able to ensure that his apprentices were listening to the sermon, and not whispering to each other.

The town authorities also made rules about pay and hours of work: they did not want to see one employer paying more to his workers, or giving more free time to his apprentices, than another employer in the same town. A master in fact could be fined as much as £5 and given ten days imprisonment if he overpaid his workmen. There were even rules about amusements and clothing.

Rules about apprentices' clothes

Apprentices must *not* wear

bright colours like the fashionable flame and peach
fashionable padded doublet and breeches
silk stockings, embroidered shirts and ruffs
An apprentice must not hide any smart clothes in someone else's house
He must not carry weapons but he may carry a 'convenient meat knife'.

Apprentices *must* wear

dull blue, russet, white, sheep's colour
plain tunic and unpadded breeches made of canvas, sackcloth, leather and wool.

Apprentices also had to wear a plain woollen cap like this one so everyone could tell they were apprentices – which they did not always like.

1 Throughout the sixteenth century Parliament passed laws making rules like these about what people should wear. In 1583 a writer complained that it was difficult to tell 'who is noble, who is worshipful, who is gentleman, who is not'. Do you think, therefore, that these laws were strictly obeyed?
Would Richard wear these sorts of clothes anyway? If so, why?

2 Why did the town authorities make rules about pay and work hours?

At the end of his seven years of apprenticeship Richard finished his training as a glovemaker; he could then earn his living by hiring himself out by the day, either to his own master or to another glover. He would become a journeyman (from the French word *journée*: day or day's work). If he then worked really hard, he might eventually save up enough money to set up his own business, though before he did so he would have to pay an entrance fee to the Glovemakers' Company – the guild to which all the town's glovemakers belonged. But he would be very lucky if he managed this. It would be hard to save up enough money for the entrance fee, and even if he did, the glovemakers in the town were unwilling to allow new shops which might take away their trade.

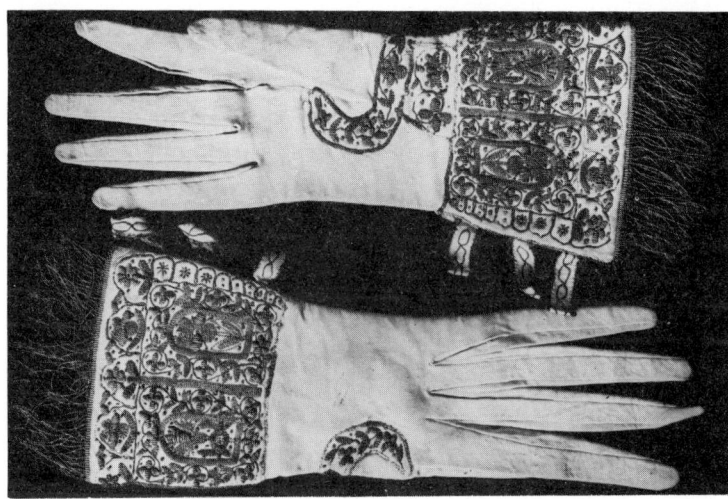

These beautifully decorated gloves belonged to Queen Elizabeth I. Fashionable gloves were very popular and were often made of such fine materials as velvet and satin, and the best leather – kid, doeskin and suede. Sometimes people wore two or three pairs of gloves, one over the other. Richard Greene would probably learn to make plainer gloves for John Procter's customers.

Country children

Richard often thought about his family who lived in a small village five miles away. Although it was not far, he had few chances to walk to see them; but he knew things were not going well. When he had become an apprentice two years before, his father, Will Greene, had been able to scrape together the £10 needed to give John Procter in return for the training his son would receive. At that time Will had been a successful small farmer. He grew enough crops, and kept enough cows and pigs, to feed his family and have a bit extra to sell. But he did not own his land, and could be thrown off it if the landlord chose. This is just what had happened; the landlord had taken back most of the land for sheep farming.

Like most of the villagers, the Greene family now only had their cottage and a small garden. They could not grow all they needed there, so Will Greene had to try to make a living by working for other people. In bad times he could find no paid work – anyway, the landlord's sheep needed only a few shepherds to care for them, so there was little work now in the village. Will

Greene was worried in case the landlord took common land too. If that happened he did not know where he would keep the two pigs and the old cow he still owned.

So life was hard for the Greene family now. Richard had been at school until he started his apprenticeship, but his younger brothers and sisters had had to go to work as soon as possible. From the age of about six onwards, they had been employed around the village at weeding, bird scaring, stone gathering, sheep guarding, and any other jobs they could pick up from their neighbours.

At home there was always wood to be gathered for fuel, and babies to be minded. The girls helped with the spinning and weaving, as well as with the washing and cooking. They also picked rushes at the river side, to dip in melted fat to make rush lights.

In a good year the family was able to find just enough to eat. Occasionally there was meat – from their pigs or hens – and they could rely on what was called 'white meat' (milk, butter, cheese and eggs). But when harvests were bad they often went very hungry indeed; they had to search for nuts, berries and nettles to eat, and made a rough bread out of a mixture of oats, beans and peas.

Stocks used to punish beggars.

Very poor children

Evening was drawing in as Walter was making his way home. He passed the stocks in the market square, where one of the newly-arrived beggars and his nine-year-old son were glumly sitting. Walter threw a rotten apple at them without thinking; but then he looked more closely at the boy, and couldn't help feeling sorry for him because he was so obviously ill and hungry. Walter knew it was against the law to beg without permission; in fact, the town had just made a rule that all beggars must wear badges; but what could you do if you had no money and no food? Walter's father, although he was not very rich, had given money to help build an almshouse, a place of shelter for sick and old people, and children who were really poor. Walter hoped that the boy might end up there. He broke into a run as he reached his own street, trying hard to forget what he had seen. As he went into the kitchen he found his mother and Kate preparing supper, and full of talk about the new baby they had just seen.

Measures against beggars

In sixteenth-century England we know that people were very worried about the poor, because a great many rules and regulations were made, like these:

> **Ipswich, 1557:** No children of this town shall be permitted to beg, and such as shall be admitted thereto shall have badges.

> **Act of Parliament, 1572:** [Beggars were to be] burned through the gristle of the right ear with a hot iron of the compass of an inch about *manifesting* [making plain] his or her roguish kind of life.

Another Act of Parliament in 1531 ordered 'vagabonds or idle persons' to be tied to the end of a cart naked and beaten with whips till their bodies were bloody.

The same Act said that young persons under the age of 14 caught begging were just to be whipped, but that if they were the children of beggars who had been convicted they were to be sent to local householders as servants or apprentices until they reached the age of 24 (boys) and 18 (girls).

Helping the poor

The important citizens of Norwich did not only think up punishments for the poor. They also made plans for children of very poor parents and for orphans. Special women were appointed, whose task was to take into their homes 'the most poorest children whose parents are not able to pay for their learning'. These would be taught to read and write, and would be instructed in the crafts of spinning and carding. We know some facts about the poor children of Norwich because the citizens made a list of poor families in 1570. Here is part of it:

> Richard Rich of the age of 35 years, a *husbandman* which worketh with Mrs Cautrell and keepeth not with his wife (but at times) and helpeth her little. And Margaret his wife of the age of 40 years she spins *white warp* [see p. 32] and Joan her daughter, of the age of 12 years, that spins also the same. And Simond her son of the age of 8 years that goes to school. And Alice and Faith the eldest of the age of 8 years and the other of the age of 3 years.   *farm worker*

> Peter Browne a cobbler of the age of 50 years and hath little work. And Agnes his wife of the age of 52 years that worketh not, but have been sick since Christmas (but in health now) she spins white warp having three daughters, the one of the age of 18 years, the other of the age of 14 years, and the other of the age of 13 years, the which all spin when they can get it, but now are without work.

> Robert Rowe of the age of 46 years, *glazier*, in no work, and Elizabeth his wife that spin white warp and have five children, 2 sons, the eldest of the age of 16 years ... and the daughters spin.   *man who filled windows with glass*

> John Tastes of the age of 40 years, *cordwainer*, that work not, and Alice his wife of the same age that sews, having 2 sons, the one of the age of 11 years, the other of the age of 8 years which both go to school.   *leather worker*

cap maker

pattens shoes with very thick soles or set on iron rings for raising the wearer's feet out of the mud

Roger Stevenson, of the age of 52 years, *capper*, but now make *pattens* and Joan his wife of the same age that spin and card, having 4 children, the eldest of the age of 12 years, the other of the age of 6 years, the other of 4 years, and the other of 3 years.

'White warp' were the woollen threads which were stretched from top to bottom of a loom. Across them the weft threads were woven. The warp had to be particularly strong and well-made.

■ Make a chart of these families, set out like this entry below.
Choose one of these families and 'bring them to life': decide what sort of people they might be and, in groups, act out the visit of three important citizens who have come to ask the necessary questions to make the census in 1570.

SURNAME	FIRST NAME and AGE		OCCUPATION		CHILDREN ages, and names if given	CHILDREN'S OCCUPATION if given. Include school
	Husband	Wife	Husband	Wife		
TASTES.	JOHN 40	ALICE 40	Cordwainer (unemployed)	sews	son 11 son 8	at school

The end of the day

The Procters were all back at home now. Mistress Alice, Kate and Meg had prepared supper and soon the parents were sitting down to a couple of fried rabbits and a jug of ale, while Kate and Walter, Richard and Meg finished off the day with porridge and the remains of the venison pasty from dinner.

Supper over, they gathered round and Master Proctor read a passage from the Bible. They all said a prayer, and the children knelt to ask their father's blessing (they both knew there would be a beating if they forgot to do that!). The Proctors also gave a blessing to Richard and Meg. They replied: 'God give you good night and wholesome rest, Master and Mistress.'

And so to bed, as the light faded away. Richard pulled out his mattress from under the counter in the shop and hoped that he would not be kept awake, as he often was, by bits of straw sticking through the canvas cover into his skin! The parents in their four-poster bed pulled the curtains shut around them to keep out the draughts. Kate and her brother, and Meg, clambered upstairs and were soon snuggled down in their beds. As they dropped off to sleep they could hear the distant sound of the watchman's cry as he went on his round.

'Give ear to the clock, beware your lock
Your fire and your light, and God give you goodnight.'

The Lisle family

In 1540, during the reign of Henry VIII, Arthur Plantagenet, Viscount Lisle, was arrested. He was suspected of being involved in a plot against the King, and the authorities seized all the family's documents in order to search for evidence of treason.

This was a sad time for Lord Lisle. But for us it was most fortunate, because it meant that more than 1900 letters, covering a period of seven years, were kept safe for future generations to study. The letters tell us not only about Lord Lisle's job as Lord Deputy of Calais, but also about a host of family matters: gifts to be sent, presents to be thanked for, people to be looked after, and particularly, what to do about the children. And this was a big problem, because there were so many of them.

Lord Lisle had an important job looking after the busy port of Calais on the French coast. It still belonged to England. English wool producers sent their bales of wool to Calais, and merchants from all over Europe came to buy them, and sell their own goods in exchange.
Use this picture to make your own plan of Calais, showing the walled town, the harbour and its quays, and the merchant ships.

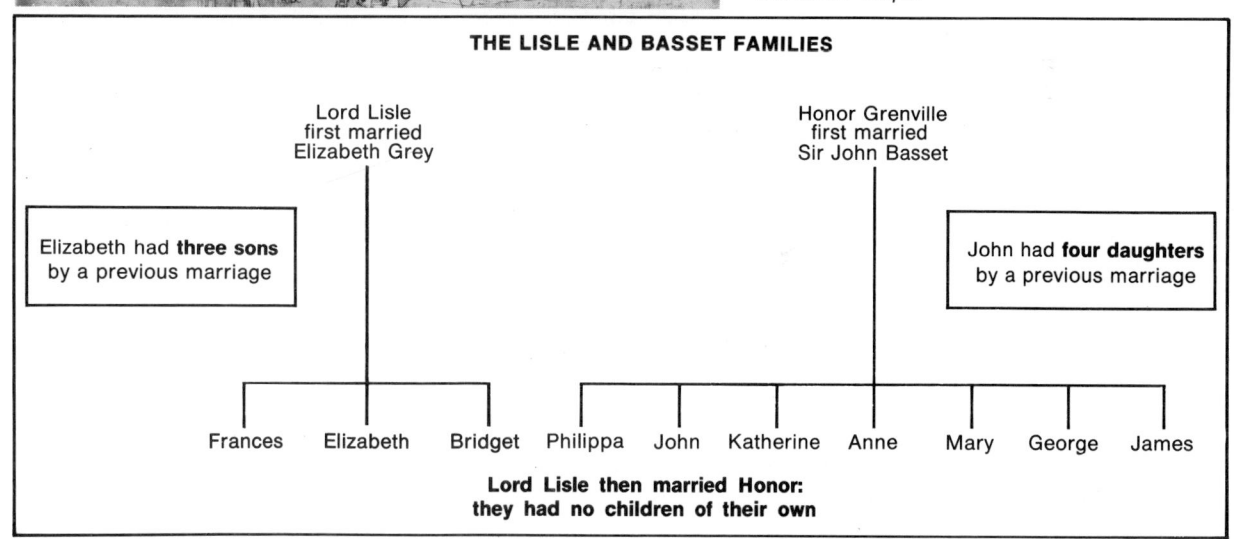

Lord Lisle had three daughters and three step-sons from his first marriage. His second wife, Honor, already had seven children by her first husband, John Basset, and four step-daughters from John Basset's previous marriage.

This memorial picture in brass shows the family of Sir John Basset, his two wives, and the children each wife bore him. After Sir John died, his second wife Honor married Lord Lisle.

1 How many children and step-children did Lord and Lady Lisle have between them?

2 Look at the picture of the Basset tomb. These brass pictures did not attempt to be real portraits, which is why the two wives look very similar as do the children underneath. Look at the family trees on page 33 and say
  a) Which wife is Honor?
  b) Which wife is shown with one child too many? Can you think of a reason for this?
  c) 'The children under the left-hand wife are arranged in order of birth.'
     Is this a true or false statement? Give reasons for your answer.

The Basset children shown on the tomb were young when the Lisles moved to Calais, so arrangements had to be made for their education.

The Basset girls

Lord and Lady Lisle made sure that, like all well-born girls, their daughters were trained in manners and domestic skills. This would prepare them for life at Court, perhaps as maids of honour to the Queen, and a good marriage. Like most noble families they sent their children away. Because they were in Calais, Anne (aged 12) and Mary (aged 11) went to high-ranking French families. Lady Lisle supplied them with clothing and pocket money. Here is Anne writing to her mother in 1535:

> Madame, I would most earnestly entreat you that if I am to pass the winter in France I may have some gown to pass it in, as I am all out of apparel for every day. Madame, I know well that I am very costly to you but it is not possible to do otherwise, there are so many little trifling things which are here necessary which are not needed in England, and one must do as others do. Madame, I have received some shoes and some *hosen* which are too small for me; I beseech you of your goodness to send me some others.

stockings

1 Why did Anne want some new clothes? Do you think she asks for them tactfully?

2 Write a modern version of this letter.

Anne enjoyed her time with the French family, and stayed with them for nearly three years. She was treated just as if she had been a real daughter of the house. But now the time had come to advance her career by getting her to Court. It seems that she was pretty and amusing, and so very likely to make a successful marriage. Lady Lisle sent presents and wrote letters to a number of influential people; and at last Anne, aged only 16, was received at Court as a maid of honour to the Queen, Jane Seymour, third wife of Henry VIII.

The official appointment lasted only five weeks, because the Queen died after giving birth to the future King Edward VI; but the King obviously held her in favour, and she kept her place at Court throughout the King's next three marriages. She herself made a good marriage in 1554 when she was 33, but died three years later. (This was a very late age for a Tudor woman to get married; perhaps possible husbands were frightened off because her father had been suspected of treason.)

Anne Cresacre was an adopted daughter of Sir Thomas More. The famous artist Holbein drew her when she was 15. There are no portraits of the Basset girls, but this picture of a Tudor teenager gives a good idea of the clothes they wore.

Her younger sister, Mary, also went to live with a noble French family, the de Bours, in 1534 when she was 11 or 12. Here she was treated, as her sister was, like one of the family. We know she was musical because the letters tell about her learning to play the lute, the virginals and the spinet. She too was very attractive – a French nobleman described her as 'the fairest maiden in the world to look upon'.

In March 1536 Mary wrote to her elder sister Philippa:

> My good sister and friend, I greatly desire to hear good news of you and of my other sisters. If I might have my wish I would be every day an hour with you, that I might teach you to speak French. I enjoy myself so much here in this country that I should be right well content . . . never to return to England.
>
> I send you a purse of green velvet, and a little pot for my sister Frances: also, a gospel to my sister Katherine, and a *parroquet* to my lord my father, because he maketh much of a bird. I beg of you, my sister, to have the goodness to present it to him, and to entreat him to send me some pretty thing for this Easter. He

small parrot similar to the one shown on page 2

hath yet not sent me anything, although I have never forgot him. . . . I pray our Lord to give you a good husband, and that very soon.

1 Was Mary enjoying herself in France?

2 From this letter, do you think she got on well with her own family?

3 Use the portraits on these pages and make a drawing of the clothes Anne and Mary Basset were likely to wear – you can colour them richly. Underneath the portrait of each girl describe the kind of person you think she was from the evidence of the letters.

Some well-educated Tudor girls

Some high-born Tudor girls were very well educated. Henry VIII employed good teachers for all his children. Princess Elizabeth, for example, was learning Italian, French and Latin at the age of nine. So, when she became Queen, she could speak to foreign ambassadors fluently in those languages. She also learnt Greek and Spanish, and was a good musician.

Her tutor said of her: 'Her memory long keeps what it quickly picks up.' Some years earlier, her father's Chancellor, Sir Thomas More, had been bringing up his children on the principle that there should be no difference between the education of boys and girls. A friend of his, Erasmus, a great Dutch thinker and writer, said about More:

Henry VIII's younger daughter Princess Elizabeth, painted when she was 13. She is holding a book, to show her interest in learning.

> He has brought up his whole family in excellent studies . . . Almost everyone thinks learning useless to the reputation and good name of women, but More rejects this idea, and considers idleness a greater snare than literature.

So More ensured that his own three daughters, and his two adopted daughters, all received a good education. His eldest daughter, Margaret, was well known for her learning. More was also unusual for those times because he did not think it right to beat his children, and only did it in fun, and then with a peacock feather!

■ Find out about another well-educated Tudor girl – Lady Jane Grey.

The Basset boys

John, the 15-year-old Basset heir, was sent to live with Richard Norton, a neighbour in Hampshire. There his education continued until it was time for him to train as a lawyer at the Inns of Court in London. This was very important for a young man who was soon to be responsible for much land and money. Richard Norton wrote to tell Lady Lisle that John had arrived safely:

> Please it your good ladyship to understand that Master Basset, your son, came to me on Friday last past, and is in good health and merry, and he right humbly commendeth him to my good lord his father and to your good ladyship, and likewise so doth both I and my wife, most heartily thanking my lord and your ladyship for your good wine. . . . I shall do the best of my little power for the safeguard of your said son, and also for his learning; wherefore I have required the parson of Colmer to be with him at my house every day in the week to instruct him in his learning, . . . Further *ascertaining* your ladyship there is no common sickness within 5 miles of me . . . thanks and *laud* be to God.

informing
praise

■ How does Master Norton show he is taking trouble to look after John?

Five months later John tried his hand at writing a letter to his parents in Latin. His manservant translated it:

> 12 March, 1534. The third day of February, worshipful lord and lady, I received from Calais your loving letters, by the which I do perceive you all to be in good health. Since I sent you my last *epistle*, these tokens I have received from you; half a crown of gold and a purse of crimson velvet . . . and for Master Norton a pouch of russet velvet, and for Mistress his wife a pair of beads.

letter

John goes on to say that he hopes his mother is pleased with his letter in Latin, which has been 'labour and pain' to him.

John's younger brother, George, was sent to the Abbot of Hyde to be educated, and then later to St Omer in France to learn French. The youngest boy, James, was already there, so the two brothers had each other for company. Lord Lisle had sensible views on his sons' education. They would need Latin in their grown-up careers because it was still used widely in official business. But it was also important to learn a modern language like French, and they could do that best in France.

This is a letter George wrote to his parents. It makes rather dull reading, but Lord and Lady Lisle must have been pleased with the polite style and elegant handwriting.

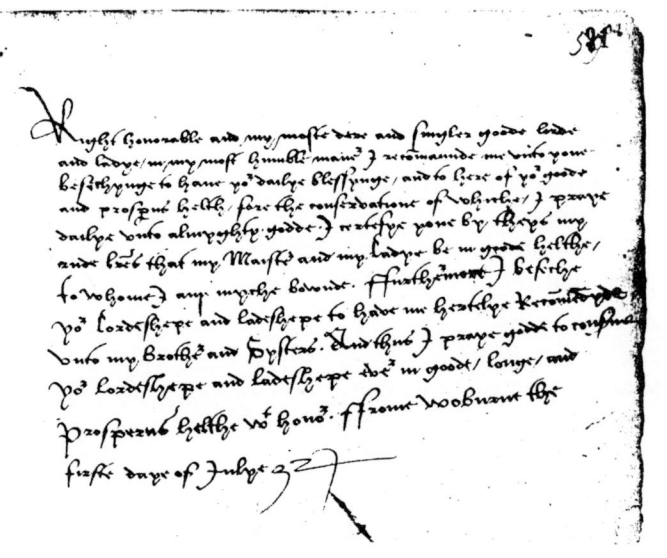

Right honourable and my most dear ... good lord and lady, in my most humble manner I recommend me unto you; beseeching to have your daily blessing and to hear of your good and prosperous health.... I *certify* [inform] you by these my *rude letters* [poor writing] that my Master and my Lady be in good health ... Furthermore, I beseech your lordship to have me heartily recommended unto my brothers and sisters. And thus I pray God to conserve your lordship and ladyship ever in long and prosperous health, and honour. From Woburn, the first day of July by your humble and own son, George Basset.

James, the youngest son, was more of a handful. He was very good at French, which he started learning at six; but he was also one of those children with ideas of their own, who know how to win over the grown-ups.

He was sent off to Paris in 1535, aged about eight, and put in the charge of some English scholars studying at the university there. They took good care of him. A letter to Lady Lisle written shortly after he arrived suggests that James should have a full-time servant to look after him:

dress
: to keep his apparel, and to *ray* him in the morning, and to see him to have his meat and drink in a due time, and to wait on him wherever he go: for they say it were dangerous that he should go alone and nobody to wait upon him: for

thugs
: there are so many *ungracious lackeys* in Paris.

Mugging is not just a modern crime!

James' guardian wrote later to Lady Lisle, explaining the arrangements made for James to move into a college:

food
: He shall have his bed alone. He shall dine and sup with the Principal of the College. And because the child is tender and come into another manner of air than he hath been accustomed unto, his *diet* also must somewhat be altered.

However, two months later he writes again to point out that James is *not* learning French as well as he might because, 'the children of the College are compelled to speak Latin, so that he cannot get the tongue there so soon as he might do.' It would be better if he stayed with a family away 'from the company of English men, or else it will hinder the learning of the tongue very much.'

So James did not stay at the college, but went to lodge with a wealthy French citizen, where he continued his studies. But obviously he was longing to get back to college life again, and within a year he was pestering people to write to his parents to get their permission for him to move. James must have won over John Bekynshaw, one of the English scholars in Paris. Bekynshaw wrote to Lady Lisle saying:

> a child of a good nature is more *pricked* to learn by glory and envy to see his companion better than himself, and that in a good college he shall have his own sort, both of birth and age.

encouraged

So, James had his way, and eventually found himself at the College of Navarre. This was a very grand place where, over the years, two kings of France were educated, and several princes and famous scholars. Perhaps the ten-year-old James wanted to impress his fellow students, because he demanded some new grand clothes as well as the college 'uniform' of a long close-fitting garment made of coarse cloth. Here is what he ordered:

Two velvet caps – one trimmed with gold buttons
Violet gown lined with marten fur
Grey satin doublet
Black velvet to make a coat
Several pairs of hose with trimmings of black and violet taffeta silk
12 shirts
Cloth slippers and shoes of leather
Chest to keep the clothes in

But it was not long before he started to grumble again:

> Madame, this shall be to *advertise* you that I have written certain letters to you, but it hath been sore against my will, and because my master hath dictated them and enforced me to the writing thereof. Very sorry I am that he should have such power over me as to take and keep from me the letters you send me, so that I can neither have sight of them nor send answer, unless it so please him. If I should be ill-handled or sick I could not inform you; for here there are some with me who have been ill a month; notwithstanding, he hath compelled them to write that they are merry and in good health. Wherefore, Madame, I would have you know that all letters which I send you shall be false, and not written of my own will, if they be not closed with my seal, as you see this one is.

tell

■ What does James say has been happening to the letters he sends and receives?
What is he going to do about it?

Later he complained to his mother that he was having to share the bed in his lodgings with a 'servant and other boys'. Although James may not have been used to this, Tudor children often slept more than one to a bed. John Bekynshaw, when he had looked into the matter, reported to Lady Lisle that James was being well looked after:

He hath with him 2 children of great houses, of his age, clean boys and prettily learned, and that boy he sent word was a servant is a gentleman's son ... a clean-skinned child. These 3 lay in one bed big enough for 4 great men ... Madame, I desire that ye will not be moved with every word your son shall send you.

1 Do you think we ought to believe everything James writes?

2 Imagine that James starts to complain about the food as well as about the beds. Write three letters:
a) from James to Lady Lisle complaining about the food;
b) from Lady Lisle to Master Bekynshaw asking what is going on;
c) from Bekynshaw to Lady Lisle giving his opinion on James' behaviour and what the food is like.

Very soon the matter of James' education was settled. Lord Lisle sent him to live in the household of the Bishop of Winchester who was an important councillor to Henry VIII. James was now well placed to be trained for a useful career. He grew up to serve the Bishop, and Queen Mary employed him on royal business.

These two boys were the sons of Henry VIII's great friend, the Duke of Suffolk. They were younger than the Basset boys, but they might have known each other, since their fathers were both important courtiers. The Bassets would have worn clothes like these.
Both Henry and Charles seem to have been clever, attractive boys. Sadly they both died as teenagers within half an hour of each other, of the sweating sickness.

Henry Brandon aged about five.

Charles Brandon aged about four.

An Italian visitor to London at the beginning of the sixteenth century wrote this about English parents and children:

The lack of affection in the English is strongly shown towards their children; for after having kept them at home till they arrive at the age of 7 or 9 years at the utmost, they put them out, both males and females, to hard service in the houses of other people ... and few are born who are free of this fate, for every one, however rich he may be, sends away his children into the houses of others, whilst he, in return, receives those of strangers into his own. They said they did it in order that their children might learn better manners. ... I believe they do it because they like to enjoy all their comforts themselves.

■ Do you think that what this Italian writer says is true of the Lisle parents? Try to find reasons in this section for and against his opinions.

A boy king – Edward VI

Born 1537, reigned 1547–53

Early days

On 12 October, 1537, Henry VIII had his dearest wish granted – a son was born to him and his third wife, Jane Seymour. The King had been on the throne for 28 years, and already had two daughters, Mary and Elizabeth. But he had broken up two marriages, and had taken over control of the English Church, in order to get what he wanted: a male heir to succeed him. In Tudor England, most people believed the country would be in great danger if a woman was the ruler; so the King was not the only one who was delighted on that October day.

So the baby Prince Edward was a very special child. Sadly, he was soon also without a mother. Jane Seymour died ten days after his birth. She had caught the kind of infection which so often killed Tudor mothers.

Hans Holbein painted Edward when he was nearly two. The little Prince holds a golden rattle, and is dressed in red velvet. What problems might Holbein have had when he painted this toddler? The artist gave the picture to Henry VIII as a New Year present.

In his own way, Henry VIII was fond of all his children, though he never had anything to do with the daily routine of feeding, washing, dressing and caring for them, and had ignored his two daughters when their mothers were out of favour. However, no father could have been more careful about this baby's upbringing and health. Wherever Edward was living the rules about hygiene were strict: the royal and private rooms all had baths and lavatories, passages had to be scrubbed twice a day, dogs were to be kept out of the house, and no dirty dishes left lying about. All the young prince's clothes, knives and spoons had to be washed after use, and all his food had to be tasted before he touched it. No outsiders from London or the countryside were allowed to have any contact with him or his attendants for fear of infection from the plague, or murder.

Edward grew up strong and healthy. He certainly looks healthy enough in the portrait above.

When he was seven months old we hear that the King spent most of a day in the nursery with him 'dallying with the prince in his arms a long space, and so holding him in a window to the sight and comfort of all the people'. A little later, Lady Bryan, who was looking after the Prince, wrote to say: 'My Lord Prince is in good health and merry. His Grace hath four teeth, three full out, and the fourth appearing.'

When he was a bit older Lady Bryan wrote to the King:

playfully

tricks

> I would to God the King's Grace ... had seen him [the prince] yesternight for His Grace danced and played so *wantonly* that he could not stand still, and was as full of pretty *toys* as ever I saw a child in my life.

So life was good for the young prince. There were kindly people to look after him and there was the love of his father and two sisters. Mary, the elder, often brought him presents when she visited, perhaps a costly brooch or a satin coat, and Elizabeth, the younger, made him a fine white linen shirt herself every year.

■ What evidence is there in this section that royal children did not see very much of their parents?

A portrait of Henry VIII at the end of his life when he was old and ill. He was overweight and had a bad ulcer on his leg. The pain sometimes made him go black in the face with agony.

Learning to be a king

Life became more serious for Edward when he was four because he now had to start lessons. He learnt to read from a horn book and was taught the two kinds of handwriting.

But even before he could read and write he practised the speaking of Latin and Greek, and was so successful that by the age of seven he could translate and compose easily in either language. In his leisure time he studied music – he learnt singing and the lute – and was encouraged to practise hawking, riding and tennis (one of his father's favourite games). Indoors, he played chess, backgammon and cards, and was taught dancing, though his teachers later tried to discourage him from cards and chess because it might lead to gambling (another of his father's favourite pastimes!).

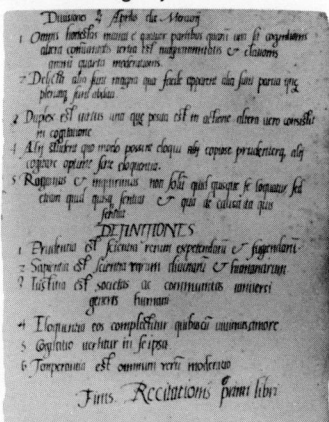

Edward was not always keen on his book work. Dr Cox, his tutor until he was six and a half, tried to make the lessons interesting by getting Edward to pretend that he was fighting a battle against the dull grammar that he had to learn. The King had been busy attacking the port of Boulogne in France, and Edward had obviously been very interested in his father's campaign – so now he imagined the Latin words to be hostile Frenchmen who must be forced to surrender.

This method worked for a time but eventually Edward grew bored and would not co-operate. Dr Cox did not want to punish him. He agreed with the ideas of Roger Ascham (tutor to Princess Elizabeth) that: '... whatsoever the mind doth learn unwillingly, with fear, the same it doth quickly forget'.

A page from one of Edward's Latin exercise books.

Edward continued to be obstinate until at last Cox lost patience and hit him. This seems to have worked wonders, and Cox had no more complaints to make about his pupil. He happily passed Edward on to his new tutors with the comment that the Prince was 'a vessel *apt* [ready] to receive all goodness and learning, witty, sharp and pleasant.': an encouraging 'end of term' report on a six-year-old!

■ Why is it unlikely that Edward would have been given a poor report even if he had been a bad pupil?

The next three years were very happy ones for Edward. His new tutor, a great scholar called John Cheke, was so warm hearted and enthusiastic that he was more like a friend than a stern master, although he could be strict when it was necessary. To keep Edward company the King chose a small group of boys to share in his lessons and games.

Even after he became king, Edward still had to continue his lessons. Cheke, and Ascham who helped him with his handwriting, made sure that he kept regular hours for work and play. He now started learning geometry and Italian, and continued also with geography, history and Greek.

He was not always well behaved. Around him he often heard adults swearing and so he started swearing, too. When told off about this, he said that one of his school-fellows had said that it was perfectly all right for kings to swear. It was decided that both Edward and his friend should be punished. But no one was allowed to lay hands on a king – this would be a highly punishable offence – so Edward was ordered to stand by and watch while his friend was whipped. Cheke, however, told him that it really was chiefly his fault and not his friend's, and that if it happened again, king or no king, he would be punished!

1 In groups, work out a dramatised version of this incident, and the conversation which Edward and his school friend might have had afterwards. You could then tape your performances.

2 Make a list of the things Edward was learning by the time he was nine. Then make a list of what you think a nine-year-old learns at school today. What would you say are the biggest differences?

Edward was about eight when this portrait was painted, not long before his coronation. He is holding a Tudor rose, the emblem of his family.

43

King Edward VI

Henry VIII died when Edward was nine years old. This picture painted at the beginning of his reign is an imaginary scene which could not of course have happened quite like this. The old King on his deathbed passes on his power to his nine-year-old son. On the right are the councillors who are supposed to help him rule. In fact his uncle, Edward Seymour, on Edward's left, seized power and made himself Protector and Duke of Somerset. He did not make a success of ruling the country, and other nobles were jealous of him. Next to the Duke of Somerset sits the man who in 1551 seized power instead – the Earl of Warwick. The picture also shows clearly that Edward lived at a time when the Christian Church was bitterly divided into Catholic and Protestant. Edward and his councillors were Protestant. The Protestant Bible, written in English, hits the Catholic Pope's head hard, Catholic monks on the left escape hastily. In the top, right-hand corner soldiers pull down a statue of the Virgin Mary, for Protestants disliked Catholic statues.

Grand occasions

Even when he was only a baby Edward had to learn how to behave on grand occasions. He did not manage very well, however, with the German ambassadors. His father was just about to marry Anne of Cleves, the daughter of a German Protestant prince, and the ambassadors had come on a state visit to the King and his baby son. They approached Edward; they bowed, and waited for him to hold out his hand. But Edward obviously did not care for these unknown German men with beards and strange, foreign clothes; he turned away from them and buried his face in his nurse's shoulder. Lady Bryan now took over and tried to persuade him to behave properly. This made matters worse, because he now burst into angry and noisy shouting. Nothing would stop him and the ambassadors just had to withdraw. The Earl of Essex who was present at the scene was delighted. He was very much against the King marrying Anne of Cleves and he reckoned that the young prince knew by instinct that these Germans were 'false knaves'.

Later Edward had to perform an official function of greater importance. Peace had been declared between France and England, and in 1546 the Governor of Normandy, who was also Admiral of France, made a state visit to England. Henry decided that the eight-year-old prince should be the first to meet the Admiral. Edward hoped it would be all right to speak to the Admiral in Latin because he had not been learning French for very long, but it seems the meeting went off well whatever language he spoke, and the people who saw him greet the Admiral were impressed by the way he coped with a situation that must have been rather frightening for an eight-year-old.

The grandest occasion he had to attend was his own coronation. As the ceremony would be seen only by a few people, the procession beforehand was made as long as possible, so that all Londoners would have a chance to view their King.

Riding on a horse covered with a cloth of crimson satin, Edward wore a gown of cloth of silver with gold embroidery, and a belt studded with rubies, diamonds and pearls. Under this he wore a white velvet doublet, and on his head a cap of the same material, set with so many diamonds and pearls that it looked like a circle of light around his hair.

Every so often during the five-hour-long procession, there would be a halt; loyal speeches would be made and verses recited, as the crowd shouted 'God save the King!' Some of this Edward must have found a little boring, but one thing he noticed pleased him so much that he asked to have it repeated. A rope had been fixed up, stretched from a church steeple to the ground:

> and when His Majesty proceeded near the same, there came a man ... lying on the same rope, his head forward, casting his legs and arms *abroad*, running on

abroad stretched out

45

Thomas Cranmer, Archbishop of Canterbury since 1533, was a quiet, scholarly man who had kept out of trouble in Henry VIII's reign. Under Edward VI he wrote the new Protestant English Prayer Book. He was Edward's godfather and an important influence on him. Edward was very serious about his Protestant religion.

his breast on the same rope, from the said battlements to the ground, as it had been an arrow out of a bow... Then he came up to the King's Majesty and kissed his foot, and so, after certain words to His Highness, departed from him again, and went upwards upon the said rope, till he was come over the midst of the said churchyard, where... he played certain *masteries* [tricks]... as, tumbling and casting himself from one leg to another...

■ Draw several picture-diagrams to show how the acrobat's tricks worked.

Not long after this show of acrobatics the procession reached the palace of Westminster and Edward was able to rest before the coronation. This took place the following day in Westminster Abbey. He was again spendidly clothed and he stood up well to the ceremonies, which went on for seven hours. The greatest moment was when he sat on the coronation seat – St Edward's Chair – and the Archbishop of Canterbury, Thomas Cranmer, held the Crown Imperial over his head. This crown was not altered to fit his head – it was thought to be too sacred for this – so a smaller copy of it was made, which Edward then wore for the rest of the ceremony. Feasting followed in Westminster Hall, where Edward sat between Archbishop Cranmer and Protector Somerset.

■ Write a letter from an apprentice boy in the London crowd to his family in the country. Describe all he saw himself and heard from others about Edward VI's coronation.

Edward's religion

Protestants believed sermons were important, because they taught people about the Bible – the word of God. Every Sunday, and sometimes on other days too, Edward listened to sermons by the great preachers of the day. Bishop Hugh Latimer was the best of them. In this picture you can see him preaching to the King, and Edward is making notes. Later he used to send for Latimer and ask him questions about the sermon.

The end of the reign

In the summer of 1549, Edward's uncle, the Duke of Somerset, faced serious rebellions in the West, the Midlands and Norfolk. The rival councillors who disliked his rule seized their chance. The Earl of Warwick was ordered to put down the Norfolk revolt. Somerset's failures led to his downfall. He was arrested on a charge of treason and executed in January, 1552.

We do not know what Edward really felt about all these events, nor about the death of his uncle. The only record we have is this rather cold and short entry in his diary: 'The Duke of Somerset had his head cut off upon Tower Hill between eight and nine o'clock in the morning.'

The Earl of Warwick who had so successfully defeated the rebels in Norfolk now became head of the Council in Somerset's place. He was made Duke of Northumberland in 1551, and was soon as important in the kingdom as Somerset had been. But he had little time to enjoy his power. In April, Edward developed a fever and a rash and was seriously ill for a few days. This illness may well have weakened him and made him less able to resist the disease that killed him 15 months later. He began to look pale and tired, although he did not admit that he felt ill.

Although not very well, Edward remained lively and active, and continued to take an intelligent interest in state business. As one of the foreign ambassadors said: 'Although His Majesty is very young, he is very able, and quite capable of understanding (matters).'

Edward now undertook a progress: he and his courtiers travelled through some of his kingdom. He hunted a great deal, ate well, and sat up late at night. When he reached Portsmouth he inspected the fortifications, and made his own plans for their improvement:

Edward would have planned a castle like this one built by his father nearby at Southsea.

> the town [is] weak in comparison of that it ought to be, too hugely great (for within the walls are fair and large *closes* and much vacant room) the *haven* notably great, and standing by nature easy to be fortified. And for the more strength thereof, we have devised two strong castles on either side of the haven, at the mouth thereof.

enclosed places   harbour

But an eye-witness felt sorry for the young king because he looked ill.

He went on to Southampton and inspected the shipyards there. He decided that too many men were being employed and ordered a number of them to go and help with the shipbuilding work at London.

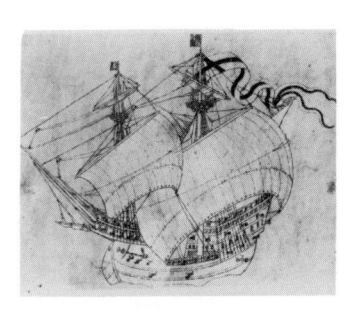

It now became obvious that he was tiring himself out, and his progress was cut shorter. Perhaps the Earl of Pembroke, with whom Edward stayed, realised that the King needed a good night's sleep on his journeys because he gave him as a present a collapsible travelling bed, decorated with jewels, which could be carried on a mule.

A typical ship of Edward's time in full sail.

Northumberland soon realised that Edward needed the help of a medical man who was more expert than the normal Court doctors. So a famous Italian doctor, Cardano, was summoned. He did not cure Edward, but after the King's death he wrote an account of their meetings, from which we learn something of what Edward was like at that time. He was, Cardano says:

> of a *stature* [size] somewhat below the middle height, pale-faced with grey eyes, *decorous* [handsome] and handsome. He was rather of a *bad habit of body* [he held himself badly] . . . He had a somewhat projecting shoulder-blade . . . Otherwise, he was *comely* [good looking], because of his age and his parents, who had both been handsome.

He goes on to praise Edward's 'cleverness and sweetness of manner', but adds the sinister comment: '. . . there was the mark in his face of death that was to come too soon.'

■ Even if you did not know, how could you tell that the doctor wrote the description after Edward's death, and not when he first saw him?

Although very ill, Edward did not fear death. He was suffering from tuberculosis of the lungs, but this did not stop him from taking care and trouble over the problem of his successor. The heir to the throne was Edward's sister Mary, but she was a Catholic and wanted to restore the Catholic Church in England. The next heir was Edward's other sister Elizabeth. She seemed to be a Protestant, but what would happen if she married a foreigner who happened to be Catholic? Protestant England would again be in danger. Henry VIII had said in his will that after his own three children the Crown should then go to their Protestant cousins, the Grey family.

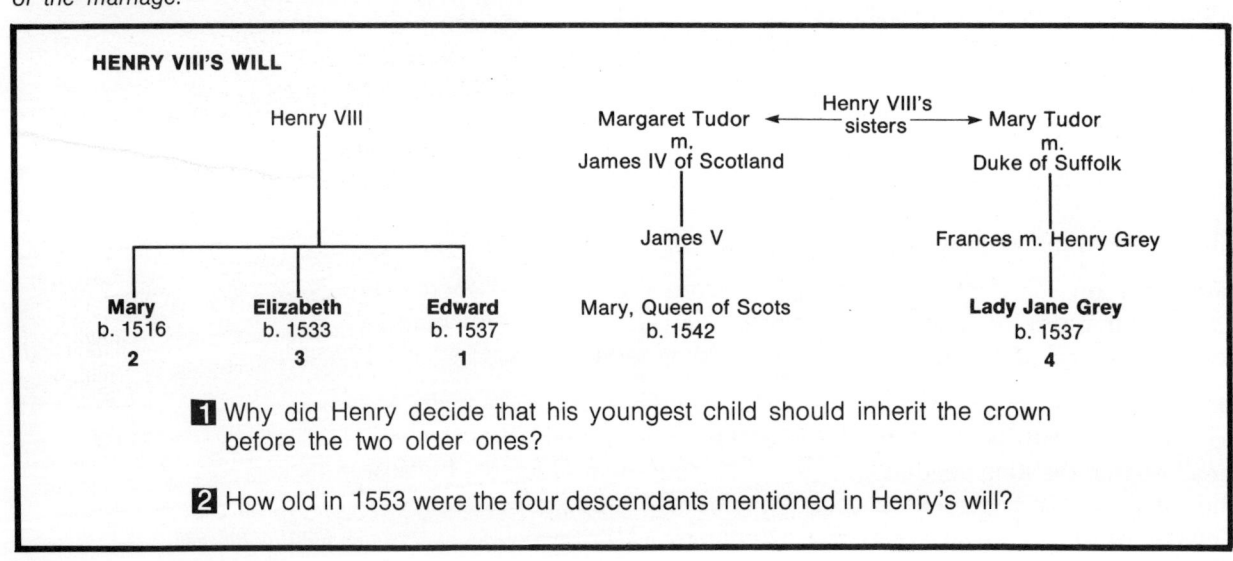

Lady Jane Grey at the age of 13. She was a quiet, learned girl and a serious Protestant. At first she refused to marry the rather spoilt Lord Guildford Dudley and her ambitious parents gave her a sound beating. She gave in only when she heard that Edward approved of the marriage.

HENRY VIII'S WILL

```
                                    Henry VIII's
                                      sisters
      Henry VIII          Margaret Tudor  ←——→  Mary Tudor
                                m.                    m.
                          James IV of Scotland    Duke of Suffolk

                                James V          Frances m. Henry Grey

  Mary     Elizabeth   Edward   Mary, Queen of Scots   Lady Jane Grey
 b. 1516    b. 1533   b. 1537        b. 1542              b. 1537
    2          3         1                                    4
```

1 Why did Henry decide that his youngest child should inherit the crown before the two older ones?

2 How old in 1553 were the four descendants mentioned in Henry's will?

Edward was fond of his sisters. But he was very anxious that the country should remain Protestant. This is part of a prayer he made up himself when he was desperately ill – he was too weak to hold a pen, so his teacher, Cheke, wrote it down:

> Lord, I commit my spirit to Thee. O! Lord, thou knowest how happy it were for me to be with Thee: yet send me life and health, that I may truly serve Thee. O! Lord God, bless Thy people. . . . O! my Lord God, defend this realm from *papistry*, and maintain Thy true religion.

papistry — Catholic Church

Probably the sick young King and the ambitious Northumberland thought out together a new plan or 'Device'. This set aside Henry VIII's will, and made Lady Jane Grey Edward's heir. Northumberland knew he would lose power if the Catholic Mary came to the throne. So he strengthened his own position by arranging for one of his sons, Lord Guildford Dudley, to marry Lady Jane Grey.

The young King's illness grew worse. He coughed almost continuously, his fever was high, and his body became covered with ulcers. His medicines were no help – not surprisingly when you look at the prescription for this one: skin a nine-day-old pig and cut into quarters. Cook gently with spearmint, red fennel, liverwort, red turnip, celery, nine dates, raisins, mace and cinnamon. Put in glass container and leave in sun nine days. Dose: nine spoonfuls.

Edward suffered terribly at the end – Northumberland seems to have deliberately ordered the doctors to keep him alive, to give time for the 'Device' to be officially accepted. He may have been given arsenic, a poison which briefly revives a sick person before it kills. 'I am glad to die,' whispered Edward to his old teacher, John Cheke.

He was three months away from his sixteenth birthday when he died on 6 July 1553.

■ What is your impression of Edward VI's character? What kind of grown-up king do you think he would have been if he had lived?

The artist William Scrots painted Edward when he was 14, just before he became ill. We can begin to see what he would have looked like as a grown-up. He stands just as his father did in one of the old king's most famous portraits. The picture is intended to show that although Edward is only a slightly-built teenager, he is also the crowned King of England.

49

Find out more for yourself

The Countess of Leicester and her children, painted in 1596.

At the beginning of this book we imagined what it might be like if the children in the picture of the Cobham family on page 2 came to life. The Countess of Leicester and her family lived at Penshurst Place, a beautiful house in Kent which is still almost the same as it was when these children grew up there. If you live near enough, you might be able to visit this house, and you may be able to find out more about this family.

In any case, you could use what you have learnt from this book to bring this family to life. Imagine that they step out of the picture, and live through an ordinary day in their lives.

Some other suggestions

1. Find some more letters about the Basset children and their parents in *The Lisle Letters,* edited by Muriel St Clair Byrne, selected by Bridget Boland (Secker and Warburg, 1983).
2. Find out what happened after Edward's death, especially to the two teenagers Lady Jane Grey and Princess Elizabeth. Many textbooks will give you information, including *A World of Change* and *Elizabeth and Akbar*.
3. There are some beautiful miniatures in this book, on page 25 and page 40. They are tiny pictures, often not much bigger than a 10p piece. You can find out more about how they were painted in *A World of Change* page 126 and *Elizabeth and Akbar* page 22. You could try making a miniature yourself.

Index

Anne of Cleves 45
apprentices 27, 28, 29
Arden of Feversham 19

babies 20-3
baptism 23
Basset family 35-40
bear-baiting 17, 18
beggars 30, 31
Brandon, *see* Suffolk, Dukes of
Bruegel 2 and cover
bull-baiting 17, 18

Calais 33
Cheke, John 43, 49
childbirth 20-1
christening 23
Clement, Francis 2, 5, 7
Cobham family 2
country children 29-30
Cox, Dr 42-3
Cranmer, Thomas 46
Cresacre, Anne 35

death, (children) 22
dress: apprentices, 28
       boys 23-5, 39
       girls 23-5, 35

education, 3-10

Edward VI 41-9
Elizabeth, Princess 22, 36, 41, 42, 48, 50
entertainments 17, 19

fairy stories 26
food 10-11, 14, 22, 30, 32, 41
furniture 11, 14

games 14, 15-16, 51
glovemaking 29
Grey, Lady Jane 48, 49

handwriting 5, 6
Harington, Sir John 12
Henry VIII 17, 33, 41, 42, 43, 48
horn book 5, 7, 42

Italic hand 6

kitchen 11

Latimer, Bishop Hugh 46
Leicester family 50
Lisle, Lord and Lady 33-40

manners 8, 12
Mary, Princess 41, 42, 48
Mary, Queen of Scots 48
meals 10-11, 14, 30
More, Sir Thomas 35, 36

names 23
needlework 13
Nine Men's Morris 16
Northumberland, Duke of 44, 47, 48-9
nursery rhymes 26

'Petties' school 7
poor 29-32
punishments 4, 30-1, 43

religion 32, 46
riddles 26

salt-cellars 10, 11-12
schools and schooling 3-10
secretary hand 5-6
servants 12
Seymour, Edward, *see* Somerset, Duke of
       Jane 35, 41
Shakespeare 19
Somerset, Duke of 44, 47
sports, *see* games
Suffolk, Dukes of 40

tailor 28
theatre 18-19
trenchers 12

Warwick, Earl of, *see* Northumberland, Duke of

Acknowledgements

The author and publishers are grateful to the following for permission to reproduce material:

Ashmolean Museum, page 29; BBC Hulton Picture Library, pages 4, 11, 13, 15, 17 and 19; Marquess of Bath, Longleat House, pages 2 and 24; B T Batsford Ltd, page 15; Bodleian Library, page 42; British Library, pages 5, 6, 7, and 31; Trustees of the British Museum, pages 26 and 33; British Tourist Authority, page 9; Mary Evans Picture Library, page 21; John Freeman, page 46; Fotomas Index, pages 14, 16 and 19; Guildhall Library, page 18; Viscount De L'Isle, VC, KG, page 50; Mansell Collection, pages 15, 22, 28 and 42; Museum of London, pages 12, 24 and 28; National Gallery of Art, Washington, page 41; National Portrait Gallery, pages 24, 43, 44, 46 and 48; National Trust, page 24; Newberry Library, Chicago, page 34; John Page-Phillips, page 9; Portsmouth City Museums and Art Gallery, page 47; Public Record Office, page 38; Science Museum, page 47, Tate Gallery, page 20; Marquess of Tavistock and the Trustees of the Bedford Estate, page 25; Victoria and Albert Museum, pages 11, 12, 13, 23 and 25; Wayland Publishers Ltd, page 5. The pictures on pages 35, 36, 40 and 49 are reproduced by gracious permission of Her Majesty the Queen.

Every effort has been made to contact copyright holders and we apologise if any have been overlooked.

> The cover picture Children's Games by Pieter Bruegel (by kind permission of the Kunsthistorisches Museum, Vienna). This picture was painted in 1560 in The Netherlands. It shows children playing all kinds of different games. If you look carefully, you will find some which are still played in school playgrounds.

A World of Change

This book is part of a series entitled *A World of Change*, intended for the 11–14 age group. The aim of the whole series is to combine a firm framework of historical fact with a 'skill-based' approach. The factual content provides continuity, and the opportunity to study causation and development. It is balanced by the two other vital ingredients for lively study of history: opportunity for 'empathy', which enables children to make an imaginative leap into the past; and study of a variety of original sources, both written and visual.

The series comprises a core textbook which studies a number of themes important in the Early Modern Age, approximately 1450–1700; a number of linked topic books; and a teacher's book for the whole series (which includes copyright-free worksheets).

The core book is primarily concerned with the British Isles, but within the context of what was happening in the rest of the world, known and unknown. The well-known political, religious and economic themes are considered. So too are the lives of ordinary men, women and children, and the way in which both change and continuity affected them. The book does not set out to be a full chronological survey, but it is hoped that it is sufficiently flexible to be used in that way if desired.

The core textbook is complete in itself, but has also been designed to provide a number of stepping-off points for 'patch studies'. Opportunities for this kind of work are provided by the eight *World of Change* topic books which are clearly linked to the themes in the main book. However, the topic books are also designed so that they can be used on their own if desired. All the topic books are listed on the back cover.

For the teacher

This book tries in a number of ways to overcome the lack of direct evidence on the individual lives of the great majority of children in Tudor England. However, the interest in family history, and the 'worm's-eye view' of history, means that there are some very stimulating books available. The following are particularly useful for the areas covered by this book.

R. Houlbrooke, *The English Family 1450–1700*, Longman, 1984

J. Youings, *16th Century England*, Pelican Social History of Britain, Pelican, 1984

M. St Clair Byrne, *Elizabethan Life in Town and Country*, Methuen, 1961

M. St Clair Byrne, *The Lisle Letters*, Secker and Warburg, 1983

H. Chapman, *The Last Tudor King*, Jonathan Cape, 1961

The *Teacher's Book* for the World of Change series also provides some further practical approaches.

© Tony Kelly 1987

All rights reserved. No part of this publication may be reproduced, stored in a retrieval system or transmitted in any form or by any means, electronic, mechanical, photocopying, recording or otherwise, without the prior written consent of the copyright holders. Applications for such permission should be addressed to the publishers: Stanley Thornes (Publishers) Ltd, Old Station Drive, Leckhampton, CHELTENHAM GL53 0DN, England.

First published in 1987 by:
Stanley Thornes (Publishers) Ltd
Old Station Drive
Leckhampton
CHELTENHAM GL53 0DN
England

Typeset by Tech-Set, Gateshead, Tyne & Wear
Printed and bound in Great Britain by
Ebenezer Baylis and Son Ltd, Worcester

British Library Cataloguing in Publication Data

Kelly, Tony
 Children in Tudor England.—(A World of change).
 1. Great Britain—History—Tudors, 1485–1603 2. Great Britain—History—Stuarts, 1603–1714
 I. Title II. Series
 942.05   DA315

ISBN 0-85950-545-6